Bread & Broth

A Bible Study For Lent

CYNTHIA E. COWEN

CSS Publishing Company, Inc.
Lima, Ohio

BREAD & BROTH

Library of Congress Cataloging-in-Publication Data

Cowen, Cynthia E., 1947-
    Bread and broth : Lenten Bible study / Cynthia E. Cowen.
        p.   cm.
    ISBN 0-7880-0710-6 (pbk.)
    1. Lent—Study and teaching. 2. Lent—Meditation. 3. Bible—Biography. 4. Soups.
I. Title.
BV85.C64   1996
263'92.dc20

                                                         95-39881
                                                              CIP

ISBN: 0-7880-0710-6

PRINTED IN U.S.A.

This book is dedicated to all those who wish to feed their spirits on the Word of God. I personally dedicate it to my prayer partner, Louise Faust, who has taught me the value of feeding my own spirit through prayer and study. Louise, who wrote and published many stories about her missionary work with her husband, the Rev. Dr. Harold Faust, in Tanzania, Africa, has enabled me to stay focused on the ministry God has blessed many of us with in writing. She has given me understanding, encouragement, and love. May God continue to bless her in her endeavors to share Jesus with all peoples.

Table Of Contents

Introduction

In the Old and New Testaments we find many references to breaking bread together as a sign of fellowship. Lent is that time when we gather as a community to be fed by our Lord through study and in many congregations through an actual meal. God and two angels visited Abraham and Sarah by the great trees of Mamre (Genesis 18). Abraham hurried to prepare a meal for his guests to feast on. As he served them bread and a roasted calf, he heard the Lord give him a promise of a son to be born. Jesus broke bread with his disciples and friends on many occasions. As they shared in a meal, Christ's followers heard their Master speak many promises. As we come together in this time of sharing a meal of bread and soup, we will be fed as a community with food and spiritual promises from this Bread & Broth Bible Study. Our Lord has given us the promise of eternal life and his sacramental meal of bread and wine to remember him by. This resource will enable us to recall the promises given in the Old and New Testaments through the study of Scripture. Coming together for a meal before the study will enable the community to get to know one another as family in Christ.

May your Lenten journey be one of great nourishment as you feast on the Word of God and have communion with our Lord and one another in a fellowship meal.

Bread & Broth
Fellowship & Bible Study

Welcome and Grace

Fellowship Meal: List each SOUP OF THE DAY

Opening Remarks
L: Lent — the season on the church calendar set aside as a time to prepare for Holy Week and Easter. Lent — a time to reflect on Jesus' temptations in the wilderness, his public ministry, his preparation for his death and resurrection, and the fulfillment of God's purpose in bringing about salvation. During this season, we often participate in certain Lenten disciplines for spiritual growth: fasting, giving up certain foods, adding more prayer time to our daily walk with God, studying the Scriptures, extra worship, and specific actions to others. Lent is a time to prepare for Good Friday and Easter, for we cannot experience the Risen Christ until we go to the Cross of Calvary and look upon Jesus the Savior. One way to grow closer as a community is to break bread together in a meal and to study the Word of God as a group. This Bread & Broth Lenten Bible Study & Fellowship Meal will give us that opportunity. So let us begin with an opening litany and prayer.

Litany
L: Dear Lord, you call us to live in union with you and with one another.
C: THANK YOU FOR THE OPPORTUNITY TO COME TOGETHER AS THE BODY OF CHRIST.

L: Jesus, you broke bread with many as you journeyed through your days here on earth.

C: LORD, AS WE BREAK BREAD, BE ONE WITH US.

L: Sharing a meal helps us to be reconciled to one another in peace.

C: JESUS, IN SHARING YOUR MEAL, WE ARE RECONCILED TO YOU AND PEACE IS RECEIVED.

L: Draw us closer to you, Dear Lord, and to one another as we feast upon the gifts you have prepared for us now in the study of your Word.

C: JESUS, NOURISH US WITH YOUR WORD AND FILL US WITH YOUR LOVE.

L: Prepare us now, O Lord, to be fed with the true Bread of Life as we come to break bread with you.

C: OPEN OUR HEARTS AND FILL US, O LORD, SO THAT WE MIGHT KNOW OUR SALVATION. AMEN.

Opening Prayer

L: Lord Jesus, help us to prepare to meet you every day of our lives. We confess that there have been times when you have spoken, and we have been unprepared to listen. We confess that we have not lived our lives totally centered on you and your will for us. Forgive us. Be with us now as we study your Word and the lives of your servants. Open our eyes and hearts, enabling us to forgive as we have been forgiven so that we might extend grace to others. Prepare us as we seek you now. In your holy name, we pray.

C: AMEN.

Bible Study: List STUDY OF THE WEEK

Closing Prayer

L: Lord, we thank you for this study and for the life of your servants Jacob, Moses, Joshua, Elisha, John the Baptist, and Jesus, those faithful who grew as they followed your will for their lives. May we continue to grow in the knowledge of your will for our lives as we gather in community and learn from

one another. Empower us to go forth and to reflect your love to others. Until we all sit at the heavenly table and eat with Jesus and the host of heaven, we give you thanks for the fellowship we have enjoyed this night as your followers. In your name, Lord Jesus, we pray.
C: AMEN.

Jacob And Lentil Stew

Introductory Remarks

Lent: the season on the church calendar set aside as a time to prepare for Holy Week and Easter. Lent: a time to reflect on Jesus' temptations in the wilderness, his public ministry, his preparation for his death and resurrection, and the fulfillment of God's purpose in bringing about salvation. During this season, we often participate in certain Lenten disciplines for spiritual growth: fasting, giving up certain foods, adding more prayer time to our daily walk with God, studying the Scriptures, extra worship, and specific actions to others. Lent is a time to prepare for Good Friday and Easter, for we cannot experience the Risen Christ until we go to the Cross of Calvary and look upon Jesus the Savior. And so, we begin this Lenten journey meeting in fellowship and studying the Word of God.

Let us pray: Lord Jesus, help us to prepare to meet you every day of our lives. We confess that there have been times when you have spoken, and we have been unprepared to listen. We confess that we have not lived our lives totally centered on you and your will for us. Forgive us. Be with us now as we study your Word and the life of your servant, Jacob. Speak to us through the power of your Holy Spirit. Open our eyes and our hearts, enabling us to forgive as we have been forgiven. Prepare us as we seek you now. In your holy name, we pray. Amen.

Bible Study

Webster defines "prepared" as the act of fitting, adapting or qualifying beforehand for a particular purpose, end, or condition; to make ready. In this Lenten study, we will look at becoming prepared as we study the biblical figures of Jacob, Moses, Joshua, Elisha, John the Baptist, and Jesus Christ.

Our first study will be on the biblical patriarch, Jacob. **What is a patriarch?** A patriarch is a father and ruler of a family or tribe; a venerable old man; a veteran; a person regarded as father or founder. When we look at the patriarchs in the Bible, we tend to view them as strong individuals, committed men of God. Examining Jacob's early life, we find an entirely different person. **What happened to him to bring about the change that caused him to be revered as an honored patriarch?** It didn't happen overnight for him, and it doesn't happen overnight for us as we seek to follow God's plan for our lives.

Jacob was third in the line of venerable old men. His father was Isaac, his grandfather, Abraham. Grandfather Abraham heard God's call to leave the security of his homeland and family and journey to the land of Canaan. God promised him that if he obeyed, a mighty nation would come from his line. *(Read Genesis 12:1-3.)*

Isaac was the child of promise whom God blessed with Father Abraham's blessing. *(Read Genesis 26:1-6.)* Son Isaac married Rebekah, who bore him twin sons, Esau and Jacob. Isaac lived out his faith before his sons as his father, Abraham, had done. But each of us has to know God in a personal way not through our parents or grandparents. Each has to encounter God, and God is always at work preparing us for that encounter. This is not to say that there will not be times when we have lapses. Abraham and Isaac both did, but they returned to God even stronger in their faith after these times.

Today we ate lentil stew. Let's look at how this soup fits into our study. *(Read Genesis 25:27-34.)* **What does a birthright entail?** In Jacob's time it held three elements. First, the head of the family exercised priestly rights (up to the establishment

14

of the Aaronic priesthood). Second, the Abrahamic family held the promise given in Eden of Satan Bruiser, that is they would defeat and strike the heel of Satan (the snake in Genesis). And third, Esau, as first born, was in the direct line of the Abrahamic promise of Earth Blesser. Remember when God told Abraham that he would be blessed and bless others? Esau, however, sold that birthright for a momentary gratification of the flesh. But Jacob, at this time, saw the birthright through carnal eyes, also. His desire for it evidenced faith, but he was not waiting on God to fulfill the promise made before he was born. That promise stated that "the older would serve the younger" (Genesis 25:23). His mother knew this. Yet the two conspired to steal the blessing Isaac was to bestow on the first born. Isaac blessed Jacob, thinking it was Esau. *Hear Esau's lament in Genesis 27:34-41.*

The consequences of this deception for both Jacob and his mother were harsh. Rebekah would never set eyes again upon her son. Jacob fled his brother's wrath and lived the next 20 years apart from the blessing of family and outside the blessing of the covenant. During this time, God did not abandon Jacob, but the schemer was permitted to reap the shame and sorrow of his self-chosen way.

Often we go our own way, but God is still with us, confirming his promises as he was with this wayward youth. *(Read Genesis 28:10-22.)* Jacob is seen here stopping in his flight and encountering the God of his ancestors. Note verse 17 and Jacob's reaction. **Would you say Jacob was prepared at this point in his life to meet God?** Jacob had been approaching God through his father and through the flesh. He did not know this God who now spoke to him in a personal way, confirming the covenant with him. He did recognize the awesomeness of his father's God but is so centered on himself that he bargains with God in verses 20-22. **How often do we bargain with the Almighty?**

Jacob ends his journey in his mother's homeland, Haran. Here he encounters his Uncle Laban, his equal in scheming. Jacob bargains with Laban for his daughter, Rachel, to be his wife but receives the older sister, Leah. Then he takes Rachel also for another seven years of work without pay. His family grows as a battle is waged between the two sisters and their handmaidens. Jacob's flocks grow also but so do his difficulties with his father and brothers-in-law. Often our material blessings become curses when we are not centered on the one who prospers us. **How might we avoid this?**

God breaks through and speaks to Jacob once more. He is to return home. Like the prodigal son, Jacob sets out to return to his family. But this prodigal has accumulated great wealth and a large family. It is time to face his brother and ask forgiveness. As Jacob is about to cross over to meet Esau, we see him encountering God again. *(Read Genesis 32:22-32.)* **Would you say that Jacob was prepared to meet God here? Why not?**

On the eve of one of the darkest times of his life, Jacob, the schemer, must have felt overwhelmed with fear. He stood with all the possessions he had amassed under God's blessings, which now seemed insignificant compared to what faced him, and a large family, a source of joy yet also sorrow. Jacob did not know if in the morning he would be there to provide for them. Two destinies lay before him: either he would be welcomed home by his brother, or Esau would now take the revenge he sought upon Jacob. Jacob was alone. Or was he? In that night of darkness he encounters the God he had met years ago. But notice, Jacob still does not know him. He has lived 20 years apart from all who knew Yahweh. We see in Genesis 35 that his family did not know God for he had to rid them of the foreign gods they worshipped. *(Read Genesis 35:1-5.)*

This is the first recorded revival in the Bible. Jacob, who now recognizes he has wronged his brother, who has suffered disgrace and consequent fear, now obeys the God who speaks to him. Jacob instructs his household, as their patriarch, to rid themselves of all that is displeasing to God and to purify themselves to meet God. He is exercising his priestly right. **How is this done today? What do we call it? Who does it?**

16

Jacob acknowledges before his family that it was God who answered him in his distress while fleeing the wrath of Esau, and it was God who has been with him always. Here Jacob, the schemer, receives a new name, Israel, which means "he struggles with God." Communion is now restored as God reestablishes his covenant with a new creation.

Revival may prove to be God's preparation for meeting a coming test or bereavement. In the subsequent verses we find that Israel's beloved wife, Rachel, dies giving birth to their son, Benjamin. Israel comforts himself by paying more attention to Rachel's children, Joseph and Benjamin, than to his other children. **Can favoritism be dangerous?**

Israel has entered a new dimension of faith in God. As he settles in the land he once lived in with his family, he will encounter times of trial which test his faith in this God who has been revealing himself to him. Jacob's firstborn son, Reuben, sleeps with one of his father's concubines. This sin costs him his birthright later. The actions we do today will affect us and others later. Israel's daughter, Dinah, is raped, and her brothers, Simon and Levi, take revenge upon the offender. For this, they will also be cut out of their father's blessing and forfeit their birthright. Israel's fourth son, Joseph, is sold into slavery by his jealous brothers and is mourned by his father for years to come. Sin always has consequences. Israel's sons never tell their father that Joseph is not dead, but their deception will cost them later when they go to Egypt and face their brother asking for grain. All of us remember Joseph's rise in Pharaoh's court to second in command. God had a plan. Even when we sin and go astray, God is still at work taking circumstances and situations and working them into his scheme. As Joseph reconciled himself with his brothers as his father had done with his brother, forgiveness and blessing flowed. Israel joins his son in Egypt, but not without first consulting the God of his destiny. *(Read Genesis 46:1-7.)* Often we make plans without consulting God. Here we see a changed man. Jacob, in his journey from Canaan to Haran and then back to Canaan, never sought God's will. Here we see a changed heart, a man who now knows his God in a personal way and trusts in him to guide. Offering up sacrifice to God, Israel is given direction and encouragement. **How does this apply to our lives today?**

All of us can relate to the Jacob of the early years. We certainly can see those times when we have been self-centered, encountering God here and there, and maybe at times even using him and the church for our own purposes. But God continues to call us — to prepare us — to accept him as Lord. When we finally cease looking to ourselves and fulfilling our own plans and purposes, we encounter that personal God whom Israel came to know and trust.

(Read 1 John 2:3-11.) Jacob had to be reconciled to his brother. Joseph had to forgive. God calls us to love one another and to walk in a personal relationship with him every day of our lives. Our birthright as Christians is precious and not to be treated as a bowl of pottage.

God has a plan for each of our lives. We have the choice to cooperate like Israel or to walk the path of disobedience like Jacob. But God never gives up on us even as we stumble in the darkness of sin. Israel never saw the promise fulfilled but had faith that God would do what he said. He went down into Egypt as a shepherd with 12 sons. This now-humble patriarch would come into the king of Egypt's presence to be blessed. In 400 years a mighty nation of several million would emerge from there under the leadership of Moses to once again enter the Promised Land.

Israel journeyed to Egypt because he knew the God who now spoke to him at Beersheba. He went as his grandfather, Abraham, did — on the promise of God — to become a great nation. Israel was prepared for whatever lay ahead, for his God was going with him. Are we prepared for our journey? Do we know this God who speaks to us to follow where he leads? Are we willing to forgive to know God's forgiveness? Are we prepared to encounter Jesus?

Hear Christ's voice and prepare your hearts this Lent. Receive Jesus by faith and journey from the head to the heart — from Ash Wednesday to Good Friday to Easter — from death to new life. God desires that none should perish, but that all should come to a saving knowledge of Jesus Christ as Lord. He is equipping us all for eternal life and our final journey home. Receive him and begin your new life today. Amen.

Group Discussion Questions

Preparation of the Meal: When we go on trips we pack our suitcases with those things we might need. We hope that we don't encounter any problems along the way that we aren't prepared for.

How well prepared was Jacob for his quick trip?

What have you packed in your suitcase of life?

How well prepared are you for encountering God along the journey?

Share some unexpected encounters you have had on trips. How did you react?

How did you adapt to the situation?

Dish Up the Meal: When Jacob stopped for the night, he had an encounter he did not expect.

How did God appear to the young man?

Has God ever spoken to you in a dream? Share.

What promise was given to Jacob in his dream?

How did the dream impact Jacob's trip?

What are some dreams God has placed in your heart?

Did these dreams change the course of your life?

Share your dreams and hopes of making them realities.

Share the Meal: Jacob knew he had encountered God. He knew he had been in a holy place and received a holy promise. But Jacob also knew he had to be reconciled to his brother, Esau.

Why is it so important to have reconciliation?

Jesus taught us to forgive as we have been forgiven. What are the benefits of forgiveness and reconciliation?

Share how you have found forgiveness and/or extended it to another.

Lentil Stew Recipe

Rinse 8 ounces of dry lentils. Combine in saucepan with 1½ pounds polish sausage, 1 cup chopped carrots, and 3 cups water. Bring to boil. Reduce heat and cook 30 minutes. Melt 2 tablespoons of oleo in skillet. Add 1 stalk chopped celery and 1 medium onion, chopped, and cook until tender. Blend 2 tablespoons flour, 1 cup water, ½ cup dry wine, 2 teaspoons instant bouillon, ¾ teaspoon salt, ¾ teaspoon thyme, and ¾ teaspoon pepper. In a casserole dish, add this to sausage and lentils. Cook another 40-60 minutes in a 350° oven.

*If using for a large group, multiply recipe and cook in a soup kettle on low heat.

Moses And Vegetable Soup

Bible Study

Last week we concluded our study on Israel by stating that from one shepherd and his 12 sons a mighty nation would emerge from Egypt. This is a fulfillment of the promise that God gave to Abraham when he established his covenant with him. That promise is found in Genesis 12:2-3. **What does it state?** *(Read.)* God established his covenant with Abraham, Isaac, and Jacob. When Israel went down into Egypt it was with God's blessing. God would take this family and in 400 years multiply their numbers into a nation of several million.

God sheltered his chosen people, even in the midst of a pagan nation, by setting them apart. These people were shepherds, a detestable occupation to the Egyptians and a natural barrier to intermarriage. Living in the land of Goshen also separated this people from the pagan influences of the nation in which they lived. God chooses to keep his people set apart from the world. *(Read 1 Peter 2:9.)* What does it mean to be God's own people? God desires that we, as Christians, be separate, to be in the world but not of it. **What does this mean?**

And so it was with the nation of Israel in their time in Egypt. However, we read in Exodus 1:8 that a new king, who did not know about Joseph, came to power. *(Read Exodus 1:9-11.)* But even in this time of bondage, God was still in control. The more the nation was oppressed, the more it multiplied and spread. The Egyptians began to dread this people and worked them ruthlessly. **Can you see God at work in this circumstance? How?** The nation prayed for deliverance. Life was bitter. People felt used. **Have you ever felt like this? Did you feel God was not hearing your prayers?**

But God was preparing his people for a mighty work. Their deliverance would be a means of displaying his glory to all the world. God was also preparing a deliverer. **Who was this?** Moses' birth is recorded in Exodus 2:1-10. Here we see from his family background that Moses is from the tribe of Levi. The Levites were descendants of Jacob's son, Levi. This is important, for out of this lineage would come the priests of Israel. From Scripture we know that Moses had a brother, Aaron, and a sister, Miriam, who would accompany him in the exodus from Egypt. We do not know anything about Moses from the time he was brought to Pharaoh's daughter until we see him a grown man. He, like Joseph, was elevated to a position of prominence by God. Educated in the court and exposed to pagan influences, Moses had all the worldly advantages of wealth, prestige, and power. Yet, Moses is a type of Christ. He was divinely chosen to be the deliverer of his people. God could have used Moses in the position to which he had raised him to accomplish the freeing of Israel. But what happened? *(Read Exodus 2:11-14.)*

It is not recorded in Scripture how Moses came to know of his heritage. Someone in the court or even Pharaoh's daughter herself might have told him that he was a Hebrew, the son of slaves. Needless to say, Moses set out to find out about his roots. He comes upon a people in need, a people oppressed. Moses does not use his political power and influence to intercede for them but reacts from the flesh very foolishly. Murdering an Egyptian overseer, he tries to cover up the act, but he is observed by one of his own people. **Can one really cover up sin so no one finds out? Who sees?**

Moses' foolish act makes him vulnerable and afraid. Satan delights in convincing sinners that they are of no use to God. Believers also are open to this attack. But Christians are always under construction, and Moses' life was in need of reconstruction. God took this circumstance and used it to prepare a mighty man of God. God uses ordinary men and women as his agents of change, but first, there has to be a change in their hearts. Times apart with God help us to focus on this. Moses had his time apart now. Rejected by his own people and fleeing from the wrath of Pharaoh, who now wants to kill him, Moses winds up in the land of Midian. **How do you think Moses felt as he sat down by a well to ponder his circumstances? Can he be compared to Jacob the night he wrestled with God?** Like Jacob, Moses was about to encounter the God of his ancestors. Like Jacob, Moses might have pondered his sin. Jacob had sinned against his brother Esau by stealing his birthright. Moses had sinned by killing a man. Jacob had lost his family through deceit. Moses must have felt like a man with no family connection at all. Jacob lived in Haran for 20 years because of his folly. Moses had come to realize the people he had grown up with were not his own, and his own people, with whom he now identified, rejected him. Jacob did not know God. Moses did not know God. Jacob had a heritage which he left behind when he went to Haran. Moses had only a heritage of faith in a slew of gods. He had no idea of the God of Abraham, Isaac, and Jacob for no one had handed that faith down to him. **How do we receive faith? How can we hand that faith down to others? What is the value of faithfulness? Is it possible to encounter God in others?**

Like Jacob, Moses had to encounter God for himself, and that is what God now had in mind for him. During the time Moses is removed from his people, he begins a new life. He takes a bride and has children. He pursues an occupation tending the flocks of his father-in-law, Jethro. God is at work in us as we live out our daily lives. God has plans and purposes for us to fulfill. Moses did not know that God had a plan for his life. We do. God has a specific plan for each of us, and he is preparing us to do it. So it was with Moses. God humbled this once proud, arrogant man. The whole foundation of his life had been knocked out from under him. He felt apart from his people, a people he did not really know. Moses named his first son Gershom, saying, "I have been an alien in a foreign land." But it was here, as a stranger in a strange land, that God would reveal himself to his servant. This is a reassuring thought for each of us as we at times find ourselves in similar circumstances.

Moses was not actively seeking God. He may have heard about the God of the Hebrew people, but he was not pursuing him. God appeared to Moses at Mount Horeb in a burning bush. God caught Moses' eye. It is not every day that one encounters a bush burning with fire yet not being consumed. God tickles Moses' curiosity. When God reaches out to us in like manner, we should do as Moses did and approach him. The choice is ours. We can ignore God's invitation to draw closer, or we can get up and move toward him. Moses moved toward God, and when he did, God revealed himself and his plan to him.

God knows each of his children by name. The voice in the bush cried, "Moses, Moses," and Moses responded, "Here I am." Moses stood in the very presence of God, ignorant of who was speaking to him. He did not fall down before God for he was totally unaware of the Almighty. Moses was about to encounter the God of his forefathers, and this encounter would drastically change his life. *(Read Exodus 3:5-6.)* **What is Moses' reaction as God reveals himself?** God has heard the cries of his people, Israel, and he now informs Moses of his plan of deliverance and Moses' part in it. **What would your response have been if you were Moses? Can you identify with Moses in your life?**

This was a tall order coming from a God Moses had just met, and God realized this. He next gives Moses his credentials: He is the Lord, the "I AM WHO I AM." Because he is the Lord Almighty, he will accomplish all that he is presently revealing to this shepherd. He does not tell Moses how this will be done, but just that it will be. He will take this nation out of bondage in Egypt into a land flowing with milk and honey. God always sees the long-range plan and results. *(Read Jeremiah 29:11.)* These verses should help us to remember

24

this. Sometimes we become so caught up in the limitations of today that we miss seeing the overall plan God has. Moses was like this. He did not have confidence in himself and his God-given abilities. As he begins to digest all that God is telling him, Moses wonders about the reception he might have when he returns. First, he will be greeted by the unbelief of the people to whom God is sending him. Israel, struggling with their situation, groaned under their oppression and had for a long time. Faith is the only thing which helps us when we are in those long periods of groaning. Moses was going to a people who felt abandoned by God. These are the same people who already had rejected Moses as one in authority. Why should they now believe that God was sending him to help them? **Are there times when you have found yourselves in this type of situation? What have you thought? What did God do?**

Moses is prepared for the job by God. *(Read Exodus 4:1-9.)* In verses 2 and 6 we read of the staff and hand. These speak of preparation for service. The staff is a sign of God's power. It was Moses' shepherd's crook, the tool of his calling, that when cast down became a serpent and when taken up in faith became the staff of God. The staff is our consecration, our capacity taken up for God. We have but to put our lives in God's hands, and he will empower them. The hand that holds the staff of God's power must be a cleansed hand swayed by a new heart. Isaiah 52:11 states, "Depart, depart, go out from there! Touch no unclean thing; go out from the midst of it, purify yourselves, you who carry the vessels of the Lord." God's power is available to believers in Christ. We have but to reach out for it. First, though, we are to be cleansed from sin. With Christ living within, the power of God will flow through us as we live in right relationship with our Lord.

Inside his cloak, Moses' hand covered his heart. The heart stands for what we are, the hand for what we do. What we are, that we will ultimately do. God knows our hearts and has work planned for us to do. Cleansed and obedient hearts are open to God's moving. Moses was asked to be obedient to the voice which spoke to him from the burning bush. God revealed

25

the ways which he planned to move his people to faith, but Moses still had reservations. *(Read Exodus 4:11-13.)*

Moses begins to list his faults by pointing out to God his lack of eloquence in speaking. God seeks to build up and sees the good in his children. **What happens when we view ourselves as God sees us?** God knows our potential. He desires to praise us for our positive qualities and not pick on us for our weaknesses. We are too quick to point out our faults to God. Sometimes we hope we will be let off the so-called "holy hook" and ignore God's call. God had confidence in Moses to do what he called him to. Moses continued to belittle himself, and God became angry. Instead of fulfilling God's plan just through Moses, God now turns and incorporates Aaron into the scheme to serve as a spokesperson. God exhibits here a flexibility we could all employ in dealing with difficult people and situations. God will accomplish that which he sets out to do — with or without us. If we hem and haw and offer up excuses why we cannot do as God has asked, we will probably miss out on the total blessing God has in store for us. God may turn and find another to work through or assist us in order to do what he desires. And so, God sends the two brothers forth reminding them that it is he who is the power behind the plan.

Moses' preparation time was not over. Going down to Egypt, we see Moses again, encountering God in a strange situation. *(Read Exodus 4:24-26.)* **What do you think of this passage?** Circumcision was a sign of the covenant. *(Read Genesis 17:9-14.)* God here was reminding Moses of the need of his family to be in covenant with him through circumcision. We are to be in a covenant relationship with God also. **What is our circumcision?** *(Read Romans 2:28-29.)* When our hearts are right with God through the blood of Jesus, we are in covenant relationship with the Almighty. New hearts, circumcised by the Spirit, declare Christ as Lord. We are outside the covenant when we refuse to make Christ Lord of our lives by applying his precious blood to our sins. God will remind us of our need for a savior. When he does, we, like Zipporah, must do something to correct the situation by repenting. Moses was now prepared to go forth and serve God. Meeting with his brother, he discloses God's plan. *(Read Exodus 4:27-31.)* Aaron then informs the elders of Israel of the plan. They would now believe because of the signs that accompany the talk. The stage was set for a display of the mighty power of God. God would now prepare his people. This people would emerge from Egypt having seen the power of God to deliver. We have seen that power at Calvary.

Continue this week in your reading by finishing the book of Exodus. Ask yourselves these questions: Had Moses been prepared adequately? How are the people prepared? Is there someone else God is preparing along with Moses?

Our soup today was vegetable. All the ingredients that go into it remind us that we are not in this brew called life alone. God uses many ingredients called "others" to bring about the desired end. We need to caution one another that we are not the most important part of the soup. All of us, working together, serve up a delicious fare to the world, but it is God who is the key to it all. Go forth and reflect on Moses' life and call and on what God is saying to you as he prepares you this week.

Group Discussion Questions

Preparation of the Meal: God was at work in preparing Moses to be a leader.

What are some qualities of leadership that are emphasized today?

What qualities make up a good spiritual leader?

Name some leaders today.

Name some spiritual leaders.

Who are the leaders of this church?

How prepared and equipped are you to be a leader?

How did this happen? Share.

Dish Up the Meal: A delegate to a convention was sporting a button on his lapel. It read: "On Assignment From God." Moses was sent on an assignment from God.

What was that assignment?

How did God prepare him for the task which was before him?

Who did he enlist to help him?

What part did God have in accomplishing the task?

What might some assignments be that God calls his people to do?

Share the Meal: Moses felt inadequate for the task before him.

Has God ever given you an assignment you thought you could not handle? Share.

What were your reactions at first?

How did God help you to accomplish that mission?

What qualities of leadership were developed because of the assignment?

Did anyone else help you in accomplishing that task?

Share the importance of working with others to reach a goal.

Vegetable Soup Recipe

Add 1 soup bone with meat to 8 cups of water. Simmer until meat falls off the bone (1½ to 2 hours). Remove bone and skim off fat. Add 1 cup each of cut-up potatoes, celery, carrots, and rutabagas. Dice and add 1 medium onion. Add 6 whole fresh tomatoes, stems removed, or one 16 oz. can of tomatoes. Add 1 package frozen mixed vegetables (corn, green beans, limas). Season with 2 teaspoons salt, ½ teaspoon pepper, 1 bay leaf, and a pinch of basil. Cook 30 minutes until vegetables are tender. Remove bay leaf.

*Recipe may be multiplied for use with larger groups.

Joshua And Chicken Soup

Bible Study

In the first two sessions of our Lenten Bible study we have looked at the biblical patriarch, Jacob, and the Lord's deliverer, Moses. From that study we have seen how Jacob as a young man grew up knowing of his father's God but never experiencing true faith. Encountering God at Bethel, he was not prepared at that time to begin a two-way relationship with him. We saw how God was always present with Jacob as he lived outside of the covenant in the land of Haran until he obeyed God's call to return to Canaan. On the darkest night of Jacob's life, we see him encounter God and become a different man. He is going to his brother, Esau, to ask his forgiveness. Alone with his God, he struggles, and, touched by God, he begins to live in that covenant, even going down into Egypt to die.

In Egypt we saw how God prepared Moses to be the chosen deliverer of the people now called Israel. Moses, unlike Jacob, did not know his father's God. God arranged for Moses as an infant to be rescued by Pharaoh's daughter from certain death. Growing up in the Egyptian court, Moses does not personally encounter God until he has lost everything — position, power, family — and is living out his daily life and work in Midian. God comes to Moses in a burning bush. From that encounter and with continued instruction from God, Moses is prepared to be God's vehicle for deliverance.

God also had prepared his people. He had a remedy for their ills and would bring it about as they followed him.

Today we partook of chicken soup. When we are sick with a cold, many of us will use this to help us get better. Today, we will be nourished as we look at another figure God prepared and used in his plan to now move his people back to Canaan.

Joshua, son of Nun, knew the God of his people. Joshua lived in community with others who had heard of the God of Abraham, Isaac, and Jacob. Joshua was an eye witness to the power of God demonstrated through Moses. God was present to this young man. When did he encounter God? How was he prepared for that encounter? What response did that encounter demand of him? These are questions we will deal with in our study.

First we must ask: Who was this man called Joshua? What was his background? What were his credentials? *(Read Numbers 13:8.)* Here we see that he was originally called "Hosea," which means "deliverance" or "salvation." Moses later changed it to Joshua which means "Yahweh is salvation." He is from the tribe of Ephraim, the second son of Joseph, son of Jacob. Joshua is traditionally seen as a descendant of the great national hero Joseph.

When Moses came to Pharaoh's court to seek release for the Israelites, Joshua was enslaved like the other Hebrews. The Bible does not record when Joshua first encountered Moses, but Joshua, along with the rest of the community of Israel, had to be affected by what God did through this mighty man of God. In the contest that ensued, we see that the God of Israel displayed his power over the gods of Egypt. The Nile turns to blood. Frogs, dust, gnats, swarms of flies, death of domestic animals, boils, hail and fire, locusts, and darkness all were a part of the plagues which God inflicted at this time. The Lord used what was available to him naturally to convince Pharaoh to release Israel. However, he then supernaturally intervened with the death of the first born. The battle was over. Israel was released. On the night of this final event, Moses instructed his people to observe the Passover, the night the angel of death would pass over the houses of Israel.

Joshua was there that night. He participated in this new ritual, smearing the blood of an unblemished lamb on the doorposts and eating the sacrifice. He saw the beginnings of tradition formed. Joshua was there as a people were forged into a nation who would follow Yahweh out of bondage into a new land. Joshua would see God go before him as a cloud by day and a pillar of fire at night. **What kind of thoughts must have filled his head?** The display of the power of God must have strongly impacted his belief.

We encounter Joshua in Exodus 17. Israel has been delivered from Pharaoh and passed through the Red Sea. Joshua was among the several million who took part in this exodus. They have grumbled about the conditions of the march: no food, no water. They have seen God provide manna from out of nowhere. They have seen Moses strike a rock and water gush forth. They are experiencing God's care firsthand. Joshua observes how the people murmur against Moses and against God. He also observes that the going is not the smoothest as the body of Israel comes under the attack of the Amalek, a tribe with which the Israelites would do a good deal of fighting.

(Read Exodus 17:8-15.) We discover here that Joshua has been selected to be a military leader. He is given his orders from his commander, Moses. The charge: select some men and go out and fight the enemy. Moses does not enter the battle physically, but he is there behind the scenes wielding the power of God through prayer. Moses stands atop a mountain with the staff of God in his outstretched hands. Last week we looked at the staff as our capacity laid down waiting for God to pick it up. Israel was familiar with the outstretched hands of Moses. When Moses stretched out his hands, they saw the power of God unleashed against the Egyptians. He stretched out his hands and the Red Sea parted. He stretched out his hands and they were delivered from hunger and thirst. And so, Joshua goes forth obediently knowing that the power of God is behind him. He had faith in God because of what he had already seen demonstrated.

Notice in this passage that God did not send Moses up to battle in prayer alone. **Who went with him?** We know Aaron was Moses' brother, and scholars have identified Hur as Miriam's (Moses' sister) husband. As the staff is lifted up in Moses' hands, an outline can be clearly seen against the sky by Joshua and his fighting men. **What configuration might this be?** This is the first symbolic use of the cross in the Bible. Here we see one person inspiring faith in many. As Joshua and his men gazed upon the figure of their leader, they became inspired. Moses was calling upon God in intercession to protect and give the Israelites victory. **What danger might there be in this type of situation where people act as channels of God's power? How can this be avoided? What qualities are needed in a leader to handle this?** Good leaders inspire others to release their faith. **What happened in verses 11 and 12?** In the past God had miraculously delivered the nation of Israel, but we see an even greater miracle occur here. **What do Hur and Aaron do as Moses' hands tire?** Moses' comrades observed the battle and God channeling his power through their leader. They then released their faith. Taking a stone, they put it under him to sit on. They saw a need, and instead of standing around wondering what they should do, they acted. Next they took the tired hands of Moses and lifted them up. They combined their faith and power of prayer to assist their leader as Joshua and his men struggled in battle. **How might we do this for our leaders in the church today? What kind of battles are waging on our fronts? Who are those in the front lines and who are behind the scenes in our midst?**

This section of Scripture speaks to us about the power which is released by two or three gathered in Christ's name. *(Read James 5:13-18.)* The Scripture from James talks about the prayer of faith as spoken by a righteous person. This prayer is powerful and effective. One righteous person interceding can struggle in prayer at times and become tired as one does battle against the enemy. But when joined by others, the united forces will be victorious. The added prayer partners bring hope, strength, and encouragement. God prepares his people to intercede. We are not alone in this battle for souls. If you have been praying and doing battle alone and find yourself tiring, follow Moses' example: Seat yourself upon the Rock, Jesus Christ, and ask God to send you an Aaron and a Hur. **What are some of the advantages of prayer groups? Do you have people you can pray with?**

And so, Israel under the military leadership of Joshua was victorious in their first battle against the enemy, thanks, not to their own strength and inventiveness, but to the power of God released in faith through the combined efforts of Moses, Aaron, and Hur.

We next look at Joshua in another role — as an aide to Moses. *(Read Exodus 24:9-18.)* Can you imagine the privilege that Joshua was given to be Moses' servant? Aaron and Hur are left behind with the people while Moses and Joshua go up into the mountain of God. In this passage we read of a theophany occurring. God is appearing and manifesting himself in character and attributes which reveal his dignity and power. The elders see God. God first reveals himself to the people, sealing his covenant with them. Then he turns to Moses and tells him to come up into the mountain so that he can further communicate the plans he has for the governing of this nation. The leader looks over his men and selects Aaron and Hur to be in charge in his absence. But it is Joshua he chooses to accompany him. **What attributes might Moses have seen in Joshua that would have caused him to be selected for this honor?**

Joshua truly encounters God working in a mighty way. As he accompanies Moses and sees him enter a cloud, Joshua is left alone. Experiencing the glory of God, Joshua is not fearful. He does not turn tail and run. We do not know where he waited for Moses, but the fact is that he waited. He viewed the display of the majesty of God as fire consumed the top of the mountain. He waited forty days and forty nights for Moses' return. **What thoughts must have gone through his mind at this time?** God certainly had to be first in his musings. **What is the value of waiting?**

When Moses came back down, Joshua was there. *(Read Exodus 32:15-18.)* **What does Joshua think is happening in camp? Is he naive or does he think the best of people?** Moses knows what the revelry is about but does not criticize his assistant. Joshua does not think ill of others. He has waited, and here is Moses. It doesn't even pop into his head that the people might not have done the same thing. But God knew, and Moses knew. Joshua, who had been nearest to Moses, joins him on his descent down the mountain, but he plays no further role in the events that follow as we see recorded. *(Read Exodus 32:19-20.)* Moses throws the tablets of the law down, signifying that the covenant relationship no longer exists between Israel and God. He challenges all who are loyal to Yahweh to kill those who are not. *(Read Exodus 32:25-29.)* Moses institutes a purge. Was Joshua one of those who went out and slew his disloyal brethren? Possibly, for he was loyal to Moses and a fighter. About 3,000 Israelites were killed as God purged his people. If Joshua did not personally become an arm of the Lord, he certainly saw all that occurred. This prepared him for radical obedience, if he had not already been prepared. The people had sinned, but we see God's grace extended through Moses as he pleads for Israel before God. *(Read Exodus 32:31-32.)*

Let's pause and look at some of the attributes of this man Joshua.

1. He was patriotic, a partaker in his people's heritage, part of the development, in fact, of that heritage. **Is this a good quality to have? Why?**

2. He was a follower, part of the vast mob that God led out of Egypt. **Is this a good quality to have? Why?**

3. He was a leader, a military man, chosen to be head of an army. **Is it possible to be a leader and a follower?**

4. He was an observer, keenly aware of the power of God manifested before him. He personally experienced the victory that trusting in that power brought as he released his faith. **How might this be seen in our lives?**

5. He was trusted, serving as an aide to Moses, accompanying him into the very presence of God. **How do we build trust? What are some of the benefits?**

6. He was courageous, in the face of the enemy and in the face of the Almighty. He did not fear experiencing the glory of God. **How do we build up courage?**

7. He was patient, waiting for God to bring victory, waiting for Moses to return, waiting for instructions. **What are some of the results of impatience? Of patience?**

8. He was obedient, never questioning a command from Moses. **What is obedience? To whom are we to be obedient?**

9. He was an overcomer, not shrinking from the battle or from the in-house fighting. **When conflict arises, how do we respond?**

10. He was faithful to Moses and to the God he was experiencing. We could go on, but these ten qualities are strong characteristics that are valuable. **Do you think they are God-given? Do you think God provided the circumstances to strengthen them and developed the potential for them within Joshua? Might he do the same in each of us?**

Joshua did not seek glory for himself. He did not envy Moses his role as leader. He did not envy Aaron and his sons being chosen to be priests. He served Moses and the God who led his nation without asking for anything. He tended to look on the bright side of each situation. *(Read Numbers 13:1-25.)* Notice the numbers of spies who went out. They were all leaders of Israel, and Joshua was among the twelve. Leaders are always called to a specific responsibility. They are given a mission to accomplish. **What was this group's mission?** The Lord does not just turn leaders loose into the world to look for a cause to champion. God assigns leaders a definite task to further his kingdom. We often generalize, but God is specific and definite. We could do well to learn that lesson. God reveals a vision to those he has given great responsibility. He shows them what "may be" achieved. He opens the eyes of the leaders to the potential that they have to achieve. With God all things are possible! God will later reveal to Joshua the divine plan that he has for the nation of Israel, but here he is just asking them to trust him. Look at the report they give. *(Read Numbers 13:26-33.)* As a loud cry goes up from the community, it is more than just a cry against Moses and Aaron. It is a cry against God. Caleb provides a vivid contrast to the report of the other ten spies and so does Joshua. *(Read Numbers 14:5-9.)* Joshua joins Caleb in exhorting the community to believe that God is able to lead them into this new land. Their optimism almost results in a stoning by their community. The minority report was not to be believed. **Have you ever found yourself in a similar situation? What happened?** Joshua and Caleb chose to believe God would give them what he had promised. They had seen their God in action. He had brought them safely this far, so why should he now choose to kill them by allowing these giants to overpower them? It did not add up to them.

In Numbers 14:24 God refers to Caleb as a servant with a different spirit, one who follows him wholeheartedly. In Numbers 32:12 Joshua is coupled with Caleb as God states that they both followed him with their whole hearts. **What does wholehearted devotion to God entail? What are the benefits?** Because of their commitment, Caleb and Joshua would have the privilege of entering the Promised Land. None of those who had seen God's display of glory would enter the Promised Land except Caleb and Joshua. Israel would now begin to roam for 40 years, never realizing their potential. Their lack of trust in God and their sinful natures led them time and time again to pray to God for mercy. Moses would also be denied entry because of disobedience. He smote a rock instead of speaking to it as God commanded, and it cost him. But God had provided a successor, one who had been with him since the exodus until the Promised Land was in view. Joshua, son of Nun, is divinely appointed and commissioned by God to lead the people across the Jordan River. *(Read Numbers 27:18-23.)* We see here that Joshua has God's Spirit within him. It is this Spirit that has enabled him to obediently follow his Lord. As Moses' successor, Joshua would assume an awesome responsibility. **Was he prepared for the task?**

In the closing chapters of Numbers we see Moses die after viewing the Promised Land. Joshua is then compelled to face the unexpected responsibility of finishing the task of taking Israel into Canaan. "God's workmen may die, but God's work goes on," it is stated. The death of a leader is always a challenge to a nation. When one life is cut off, someone else must take that place. God is never caught off guard. He has appointed a new leader for this situation. *(Read Joshua 1:1-10.)*

Joshua now stands before his people as an encourager, exhorting them to go forward and take possession of all that God has for them. God chose Joshua to carry the torch for him and to lead his people to their objective. Was he ready? His long association with a God-inspired man prepared him now for this leadership role. God had readied him through circumstances and testings of faith. Joshua remained faithful, always carrying out the command of the one in authority. He shared confidences with Moses and had worked side by side with him. Joshua had encountered God in Moses and in all that was occurring around him. His faith was made strong in the furnace of affliction. He held tightly to the promises of God and anticipated that they would be fulfilled. Israel never realized their full potential to take all of the area God had for them to possess. This was not Joshua's fault. He led them in, but he could not make them claim the promises he and Caleb did. We are called to be Joshuas, called to see that God is around us and in us, called to take all he has for us. Our part is to be faithful and when he commands, obey. Don't give God hassle. Go forth and be overcomers. Be Joshuas today!

Group Discussion Questions

Preparation of the Meal: Jacob became a leader after God developed some character qualities in him. Moses became a leader after being given a difficult task. Joshua was a man of good character who was given an assignment to lead the people of Israel into the Promised Land. Each of these leaders has an impressive resume.

If you were on the Call Committee for securing a Christian leader for your congregation today, list what you would be looking for.

What is the importance of having a good resume for leadership?

We all have qualities that would aid us as a Christian leader. What does your resume as a Christian leader look like? Share how you might improve it.

Dish Up the Meal: Jacob, Moses, and Joshua served as role models for the community of faith.

What is a role model?

How do we model the faith for others?

What is the importance of others seeing how alive and active our faith is?

Have you ever witnessed to that faith in Christ? Share your story.

Share the Meal: Joshua received his marching orders from God: Go and claim the Promised Land. He sent out scouts to survey the territory. He gathered information and made an informed decision. Leaders need to count the cost of how to go about implementing a vision and then present it accurately to their followers.

What happens when followers ignore the leader's advice?

Have there been times when as a leader your advice has not been listened to?

How did that make you feel?

Being a Joshua today takes courage. Do you know any people like Joshua? Share.

Chicken Soup Recipe

Begin with 1 large chicken and 3 quarts of water. Add 3 stalks of celery, 1 large onion quartered, ¼ teaspoon basil, 1 tablespoon or less of salt, 2 carrots, 2 cloves of garlic, and ¼ teaspoon pepper. Cover, simmering 2½ hours until chicken is tender and pulls from bone. Strain. Remove meat from bone and refrigerate broth overnight. Skim and discard fat. Heat broth to boiling. Add 2 cups sliced carrots, 1 cup chopped celery, 4 green onions with tops, and 1 thinly sliced tomato. Add cooked chicken. Cook until vegetables are tender. Add noodles or rice for added variety.

*Recipe may be multiplied for use with larger groups.

Elisha And Potato Soup

Bible Study

Poor Vice President Quayle took a beating for the spelling of the word potato. Sometimes things seem so right, just like adding the letter "e" at the end of potato seemed right for this spokesperson for our nation, but it was not right. Today we ate potato soup. The potato was brought to our land from South America in the time of Columbus. What a blessing that vegetable has become to our diets! It is a unique food product that was incorporated into the diet of the world because of contact with foreign lands. The potato is a healthy staple, but not all contact with foreign things is healthy.

Jacob commanded his family to rid themselves of their foreign idols. They obeyed his voice, and then they met God. Moses lived all his life in a foreign land exposed to many gods. Putting aside pagan influence and obeying the voice of the burning bush, he then met God. Joshua, set apart in the land of Goshen yet exposed to the same foreign temptations, knew his people had to be warned of the dangers of worshipping heathen gods and of worldly alliances with those nations. They had met God in the wilderness, been sustained by him in daily life, and now, with his own death around the corner, Joshua challenged Israel to follow only Yahweh and serve only him. *(Read Joshua 24:14-21.)* Note in verse 23 that the people already had foreign idols in their possession. How soon they had fallen away from God! The 12 tribes of Israel had taken their land in Canaan but had failed to drive out their enemies.

Intermarriage had caused a breakdown in worship. Altars had been set up to other gods. Often conquest gives way to complacency. God had demanded extermination of false worship, yet Israel tolerated and even engaged in it. Because of their incomplete obedience, Israel forfeited God's fullest blessings. Thus we see a time of decline as we approach our study today. The generations to follow Joshua were ones which did not know the Lord and had not seen what he had done. The nation, prepared by God to be his own, began a pattern which can be traced in their history of sin, servitude, supplication, and salvation.

The Book of Judges shows how this nation continued to do "evil in the sight of the Lord." Serving the Baals and the Asherahs, they brought God's anger upon themselves for their sin. Then oppression by their enemies would follow. Crying out to God, the Lord would answer and save them. Sin, servitude, supplication, salvation. Salvation came with judges such as Gideon, Samson and Deborah, who were chosen and prepared by God. These judges would help God's people return to him. With the death of each judge, however, the nation would begin again its dance of sinning, being enslaved, praying, and being delivered. But the nation was in the process of hardening its heart to God's voice. **How is this possible for people of faith? Is there a danger for us today?**

Proverbs 28:14 warns us that we are blessed when we fear the Lord, but when we allow our hearts to harden we fall into trouble. Israel did this. There came a time when there was no mourning for sin, no humbling because of national transgressions, no returning to Yahweh. Consequently, no word came from God.

Wickedness invaded the people of God, a people he had prepared to be holy and separate. They strayed from God, but he had not left them. God saw evil taint even his own priests. He now chose a child, Samuel, to be his spokesperson. *(Read 1 Samuel 3:1-10.)* God spoke to this lad, preparing him at a young age to be his prophet priest. **How important is it to instruct our young people in the ways of the Lord? What are the benefits?**

44

What is a prophet? Derived from a Greek word meaning "one who speaks before others," we find that a prophet is one who communicates divine revelation. God is not concerned about sex here — a prophet can be female or male. Aaron and Miriam can be said to have been prophets. Moses certainly takes the lead in this department. A prophet does not just speak in the church but speaks to the community and the world. Samuel was one who was involved in the external and internal politics of Israel. Elijah and Elisha took up the role of opposing the instituted monarchy of their time. But God's spokespersons are not always accepted, just as God's ways are not always followed. The Lord desired to rule his people, blessing them and governing them through divinely chosen people like Jacob, Moses and Joshua, but Israel wanted a king. *(Read 1 Samuel 8:6-9.)* **What do the people do here?**

Rejecting God as king, Israel found that not all kings are godly. Their first king, Saul, turned out to be less than prepared for kingship. He was rejected by God when he elevated himself by intruding upon the office of priest by offering up sacrifice. David, the shepherd king, followed God wholeheartedly but had his personal struggles with family which impacted his reign. His son, Solomon, reflected the condition of the nation who still had problems with foreign objects. *(Read 1 Kings 19:1-6.)* After the death of Solomon, the kingdom of Israel divided into northern Judah and southern Israel. God was still with them even in their division. He raised another to speak for him, the prophet Elijah.

Our focus for study today is on the prophet who would come after Elijah. Elisha was Elijah's understudy. He represents that lineage chosen by God to speak for him, to communicate with him, and to reveal that communication to his people. In order to understand how God prepared Elisha, we need to look at the role model that he had in Elijah the Tishbite.

Elijah's ministry was one of public display of God's power. He spoke and drought came upon the land for three years. He prayed for rain, and rain came. He raised a widow's son from the dead. Engaging in the politics of the day as a representative of the Lord, he battled the wicked King Ahab and his equally wicked wife, Queen Jezebel. *(Read 1 Kings 18:20-24.)* Elijah was not afraid of the powers that be — political or religious. The 450 prophets of Baal did not intimidate him, for he knew this God he served. He battled evil in high and low places, but he began to suffer from a Lone Ranger complex. Fleeing for his life from Jezebel after putting the 450 to death, we find him traveling 110 miles from Mount Carmel to Beersheba to have his own pity party in a cave. *(Read 1 Kings 19:9-18.)* **What is the danger in seeking to do God's work on our own? What happens when human resources are depleted? Who is the power behind the moving of the Kingdom on earth?**

Elijah and each of us need to be freed from bitterness. Despair and isolation impact the call of God to do his work. Elijah sought comfort and encouragement, and God told him exactly what was up: he was to return and not run from Jezebel like a wounded pup. Elijah felt he was alone in God's army, but God told him there were 7,000 faithful out there. Elijah got up from his pity party and looked up to God. He now was about to be linked up with another. In verse 15 we see God giving him new work and new comrades. He is to anoint Hazael as king of Syria, anoint Jehu king of Israel, find the faithful and, best of all, enter into fellowship with Elisha. It is in the shoulder to shoulder contact with others that we are uplifted. **How might we do this in the church today?**

(Read 1 Kings 19:19-21.) Here we see the call of Elisha. His credentials and background are given. Having 12 yoke of oxen, **what might we assume his family's financial condition to be? Driving the oxen himself, what might we assume his role in the family to be?** Elisha was not sitting around waiting for fortune to come his way. He was actively at work. God comes to his people as they labor, enabling them to be fruitful and respond to his call.

When Elijah met Elisha, what did he do? There was no flowery speech. He threw his mantle around the younger man.

46

The prophet's mantle was made of skin covered with hair, probably goat's skin with the hair turned outward, a garment distinctive of the prophet. *(Read Matthew 3:4.)*

What did Elisha ask before he followed Elijah? His wanting to return to say good-bye to family shows that they were important to him. Elijah's answer is difficult to interpret. Some scholars feel it means, "I have done nothing to you to prevent a proper leave taking from your people." Elisha's desire to properly say good-bye to his family shows he honored his parents. Elijah gave him leave. But it can also be said that his answer was one of exhortation reminding the younger man that he has been anointed by God to be a prophet, and that call on his life had to be responded to immediately. The response was up to him.

Elisha responded rightly. Giving a lavish feast for his parents and friends, he says farewell and begins his internship with Elijah. We do not know what courses Elijah required in this College of the Prophets. We do not know what God taught Paul when he called him into the desert to be alone with him. Times of preparation like this are important to each of us. Like Jacob and Moses, Elisha responded to God's call, and like Joshua, he walked obediently with Elijah. Like his successors, Elisha saw the power of God miraculously displayed and learned the role of prophet, relying on God's provision in all areas of his life. **Is this important in our lives? How might God accomplish this in us?**

The two prophets must have had quite a bonding and partnership. When it came time for them to part, it had to be very difficult. *(Read 2 Kings 2:1-8.)* **What does Elijah strike the water with?** The cloak represents the power of God. Moses had his staff; Elijah has his cloak. The power of God parted the Red Sea and here parts the Jordan River. God's power applied to water is awesome. Elisha refuses to leave his master. He is faithful to his calling to accompany him. Even when told to leave, he refuses. So they cross together. Elisha knows Elijah is about to take his leave from this life and desires something of his to be left with him. *(Read 2 Kings 2:9-12.)* In this symbolic section, we see Elijah representing Christ and Elisha the Church. The mantle is the Holy Spirit's anointing. Here we see Pentecost. Elisha cries out to the master he has loved so personally and deeply as God's chariots descend. Their walk is over. Like Joshua and Moses, Elisha has witnessed the power of God operating in his mentor's life and desires a double portion, not just the same power. Elisha mourns his departure but then picks up the mantle and sets forth to carry on the ministry.

(Read 2 Kings 2:13-14.) The ministry of Elijah was public. The ministry of Elisha would be private. Here he imitates his predecessor. Calling upon the God of power, he parts the waters. This evidence demonstrates the first transfer of supernatural power. Elisha knows that it is foolish to try to measure up to the greatness of Elijah. He is called to complete the ministry Elijah has left behind. He will go to God's people and call them to repentance. Elisha will anoint Jehu and incite Hazael to murder his master and usurp his throne. Elisha will carry on the work left to him but never obtain the same heights of greatness as Elijah. **Does this bother us today? What qualities enable one to complete the unfinished tasks of others? Are there parallels with Jesus and the disciples here? What do we need to do God's work?**

Elisha's career has no stupendous scenes in it, no outstanding achievements, no exhibitions of grandeur of the soul. Yet his career reminds us that we can do much good in the world if we are obedient and faithful to the God we love and serve. Miracles do occur in Elisha's private ministry: The Miracle of Provision (for a widow, a dead son, poisoned prophets); The Miracle of Perception (reading the king's mind, opening the eyes of the young servant); The Miracle of Protection (removing the threat of the Syrian army). Each miracle shows God's willingness to do for the nation what he has done for the individual: provide, protect, and defend all who turn to him. God is great caring for us privately as well as corporately. God provides through Elisha an oil well for the destitute widow, gives new life for a dead boy, makes poisoned stew harmless, multiplies bread for a hungry crowd, cures a leprous army captain, makes an ax head defy the law of gravity, reads the mind of an enemy, opens the eyes to see angels, and closes the eyes of the enemy to the same spectacle.

In closing, let us look at *2 Kings 4:1-7*. Elisha's ministry resembles the work of Jesus. Elijah, a prophet of the wilds, appeared at moments of religious crisis, and then disappeared into the solitude of the desert. Elisha walked daily with others, interested not only in great events but in the nitty gritty of life, in the needs and sorrows of men in everyday experience. Elisha, moved with compassion, used his power to banish sorrow and to bring hope and cheer into the lives of ordinary men and women. Christian ministries should have the same qualities and goals. God calls us and gives us a new work to perform: to further his kingdom under his power. Like those we have studied so far, when possessed by God's Spirit, we, too, will perform deeds of mercy and mighty acts. This is a high calling. Moving among God's people, sensitive to his voice, we will bring courage and hope to the disheartened and bewildered. Jacob, Moses, Joshua, and Elijah may have had more flare in their call, but Elisha's ministry should inspire each of us to engage in small kindnesses, small courtesies, and small considerations. Habitually practiced, these will bring greater charm to our character and may often do more good in the world than the great accomplishments of the more dramatic individuals.

The time came when God tired of his people not responding to his voice. He cast aside the ten tribes who continued in their idolatry and wickedness. God's voice no longer speaks in Israel for no one is willing to listen. A once mighty nation, they are reduced to a vassal state. Revolting, they are crushed and deported to a foreign land, receiving God's long-delayed judgment. God is patient with his children, but we must not presume on that patience. He is a long-suffering deity, but he speaks to us to repent and return to him. We live in a precarious position when we refuse. Follow your Lord faithfully as the prophets of old did, obedient and looking to Jesus as your mantle. With the Holy Spirit's power in our forgiven lives, we, too, can witness the kingdom of God today. Let each of us continue to move in our daily work seeking to minister with the compassion of our Lord to those around us. And may the spirit of Elijah and Elisha now rest upon you in double portion. Amen.

Group Discussion Questions

Preparation of the Meal: In every major Broadway play there is the star and the star's understudy.

What does an understudy do?

How does the understudy feel when he has the chance to take the starring role?

Joshua and Elisha might be considered understudies. How did they perform when given the chance to become leaders?

How had they been prepared?

How might we be considered understudies of Jesus today?

What roles might we be assigned?

How would the critics rate our performance?

What kind of review might appear in the Heavenly Daily News?

Dish Up the Meal: Headlines read: Prophet Causes Drought for 3 Years; Fire Comes Down at Prophet's Command; Fiery Chariot Takes Prophet Home. Sales would certainly be up that day. Dynamic people and their actions grab our attention.

What are some of the headlines in the news, on television and so forth, that grab our attention today?

Who are some of the people involved?

What are some of the dangers in idolizing movie stars, athletes, politicians?

Name some people who are idolized by today's society.

How do their lives reflect their faith?

Share the importance of decreasing so that Christ can increase and be seen in our lives.

Share the Meal: People like Mother Teresa, President Jimmy Carter, Charles Colson, and others have honor with our generation because of the service they do in feeding the hungry, giving shelter to others, and sharing the gospel in prison. Their ministry is public yet private. They are people who have recognized their own sinfulness and turned their lives over to God, seeking to do his will.

Name some ministries that are occurring in our nation and in our church that are done to help others.

How might we serve our neighbors better?

Is it important to have the Elijahs (public) and the Elishas (private) in life?

Is there a place for both?

Would you label your personal ministry public or private? Why?

How do you fit into furthering the Kingdom of God in your daily life?

Potato Soup Recipe

Peel and cook 15 average potatoes. Mash or put through a coarse sieve. Saute 1 medium onion cut fine in 2 tablespoons butter. Add potatoes, 3 stalks celery, cut fine (or ½ teaspoon celery salt), 2 carrots, and 2 slices fried bacon to kettle. Season with 1 teaspoon salt and ¼ teaspoon pepper. Cover mixture with 4 cups water and 1 cup milk. Simmer until blended.

*Recipe may be multiplied for use with larger groups.

John The Baptist And Beef Barley Soup

Bible Study

Last session we looked at the role of the prophet in the life of the nation of Israel. Prophets were God's spokespersons, men and women who revealed the word of God to his people. We saw how Israel had forgotten the God who had delivered them and we looked at the pattern of sin, servitude, supplication, and salvation that began to develop in their life. Eventual judgment came as they were led into captivity. Yet God was always there holding out hope to bring them back home again. Eventually, that hope was realized as they returned to Zion, rebuilt the Temple, and began to rebuild their personal lives, their nation, and their religious system.

God continues to prepare his people. He was about to intervene once again in the history of the world. Israel now moaned under the yoke of the Roman Empire. As their ancestors had done in Egypt and down through history, they cried out to God for their Messiah, their savior, to come and rescue them.

The geographically and politically divided nation had even more divisions in it religiously. Four distinct sects offered up their vision of Messiah and the rules by which one should worship God. The priestly Sadducees used their prestige and political influence to adapt to Roman rule. The self-righteous Pharisees saw Judaism as a religion centered on the observance of the law and its strict interpretation. The militant Zealots represented the extreme of fanatical nationalism looking for a military Messiah like King David who would free them from Roman domination. The devout Essenes chose to separate themselves from society, living in isolated community in order to remain pure. Devoting themselves to the study of Scriptures and prayer, they looked for Messiah to be a great teacher.

Today we ate beef barley soup. Our cooks put many ingredients in this soup which enhanced the flavor and gave bulk to make a hearty meal. God was about to stir the brew on earth, calling a separated people to come back together and return to him. He needed a spokesperson once more to prepare the way for what he was about to do, and we see him select a voice to speak for him in Mark 1:1-7. *(Read.)* Who is this messenger from God? What does he dress like? Through his appearance and diet, John made a visual protest against self-indulgence. His message was of a baptism of repentance for the forgiveness of sins. Where did he come from? How had God prepared him for the challenge that lay before him? Let's look at some Old Testament passages to find some clues.

In Mark's passage we find the Old Testament prophets Malachi and Isaiah quoted in verses 2-3. *(Read Malachi 3:1-4.)* Malachi's name means "my messenger." He was the last prophet of grace in the Old Testament until John appeared 400 years later. The final message of this fifth century B.C. prophet contains the prophecy of the ministry of John the Baptist. Christ himself will bear witness to this prophecy in Matthew 11 and Luke 7.

The Hebrew word, *mal 'aki,* normally used of a priest or prophet, meant "the Lord will come." The messenger of the covenant is Christ. In verses 3 and 4 we see that this final messenger will come to purify and judge, but God will mercifully send one before him, that is "my messenger" of verse 1, who will prepare the people. As Elijah came before Elisha (whose ministry was one of judgment and redemption) so "Elijah" (John) would be sent to prepare God's people for the Lord's coming.

John the Baptist would minister in the spirit and power of Elijah. *(Compare Luke 1:17, Matthew 11:13-14, 17:12-13, and Mark 9:11-13.)* Malachi reveals God in several relationships to Israel in this prophecy: as parent, Lord, God, and judge. In verse 3 we see that those who are supposed to be messengers of the Lord and who serve the altar as priests will be purged of their sins and unfaithfulness. A purge was needed in Israel.

Turn now to Isaiah 40:3. *(Read.)* This eighth century B.C. prophet also refers to John as the voice. "Prepare the way" means to clear all obstacles out of the road. It was an ancient Near Eastern custom that when a king would make a journey to a distant country, he would send out representatives who would make sure the roads he would travel on were clear and improved. The picture we see in this Scripture is that of preparing a processional highway for the Lord's coming to his people. John's message in Matthew 3:1-8 presents the same picture. *(Read.)* Repentance prepares the way for Christ. **What does repentance mean? How do we open ourselves to the message from God?**

Receptive minds, hearts, and ears enable us to hear God's voice. Then we become the crying voice to others looking for salvation. We make God's paths straight when we bring the creative Word to a world dying for lack of it. We go before the Lord when we help remove the things like greed, pride, hatred and prejudice which block God's entrance into this world. *(Read Isaiah 35:8.)* This highway refers to the way set apart for the redeemed of the Lord. In ancient times, certain roads between temples were open only to those who were ceremonially pure.

The Gospel of Mark begins with the public ministry of John. John's name means "the Lord is gracious." He acquires the name "Baptist" or "Baptizer" because of his practice of baptizing those who came to him for repentance. This characterized his ministry. John's message of turning from sin to righteousness was not new. The prophets of old had preached it. John's audience was not unfamiliar with it. They knew Gentile converts had to be baptized, but they had not heard that they as descendants of Abraham needed to repent and be baptized also.

In verse 4 of this passage, **where does John's ministry begin?** This desert was an arid section west of the Dead Sea. John's wilderness life enabled him to remain uncontaminated by the legal impurity of life in the towns and cities around him. The wilderness is symbolic of the center of religious hope as well as a place of refuge. Here people were prepared to meet God. **What kind of wildernesses might we have where we go to meet God today?**

God had tabernacled, lived with, Israel for 40 years in the wilderness before they entered the Promised Land. The Essenes lived in the very heart of this community wilderness. They were busy preparing the way through the study of the law and strict obedience to all that had been revealed to them by the prophets. Some scholars feel John belonged to or was influenced by this community.

How might one react to the appearance of John? What did his diet and dress say to a corrupt society? John was not just an ascetic, that is one who practices the doctrine of self-torture or self-denial to discipline himself in order to reach a higher state, spiritually or intellectually. John was a legal purist, and he certainly must have been a curious subject to observe.

The stage was set and the major characters in place. God would now begin to unfold the drama. *(Read Mark 1:5.)* **Who were the crowds and what were they doing?** Excitement had spread throughout the countryside as the multitudes heard about this young "Elijah" who was preaching and baptizing. The people knew the prophecies concerning the prophet who would prepare the way for Messiah. They anticipated Messiah's approach as well as his judgment. God had prepared the people and the prophet. **But where had this prophet come from?** *(Read Luke 1:5-7.)*

Who were John's parents? From what line had they come? What were they like? Descended from the priestly lineage of Aaron, we find that this couple lived upright and blameless lives. They were not sinless but were faithful people trying to keep God's ordinances. However, they had no children. In those times being childless not only deprived couples of

56

personal happiness, but it was also considered to be an indication that divine favor was being withheld. This often brought social reproach. **Can you recall other Old Testament women who suffered from this reproach?** (Sarah, beyond childbearing age, gave birth to Isaac; Rebekah bore twin sons, Esau and Jacob, in response to Isaac's prayer in Genesis 25:21; Rachel, battling with sister Leah, finally had her womb opened to bear Joseph; Hannah prayed to God in 1 Samuel and gave birth to Samuel, whom she consecrated to the Lord's service.)

(Read Luke 1:8-14.) Today is Zechariah's big day. Chosen by lot he is to have the honor of supplying the incense for morning and evening sacrifices. After entering the temple, **whom does he encounter? What is his reaction?** Fear grips his spirit. Human nature shrinks before divine glory. Yet Zechariah is reassured that God has heard his prayer. **What was that prayer?** A child — Elizabeth would bear a son and his name would be John. He would be a source of great joy, not only to them, but to others. Again we see a motif repeated: a child born to aging parents, the announcement of the birth by an angel, the divinely chosen name (examples: Isaac, Samson, Samuel, and now John).

(Read Luke 1:15-17.) **What will John be forbidden to do?** *(Read Numbers 6:1-4.)* Like Samson and Samuel, John is to be subject to the Nazarite vow of abstinence from alcohol. He will be prepared in this manner to be a ready instrument for the Lord, self-controlled and pure, consecrated for supreme service. Into such a vessel the Holy Spirit would come completely. John would not be operating under his own power but under the power and guidance of the Holy Spirit of God.

In Luke 1:17 we find that John is not Elijah returning in the flesh, but he would function like the Old Testament preacher of repentance and thus fulfill Malachi 4:5-6 of turning the hearts of the fathers to their children. Burning with divine fire, John would speak out with flaming conviction as he was caught up in communion with God, becoming one with his Lord in carrying out the plans of the Most High.

(Read Luke 1:57-66.) Recall the circumcision story in Exodus with Moses from our earlier study? The sign of the covenant is again made as the baby is brought for the rite. Normally the child takes the name of grandfather or father, so those assembled are shocked when the name John is selected. The significance of the new name is important, for God was about to do a new work in his world through this infant. This child of hope and promise would come to a people prepared to receive him. In this passage, the people recognize God is about to do a mighty work and anticipate a move from God. **What is the potential of a life dedicated totally, like John's, to serving God? How might we become consecrated to God?**

(Read Luke 1:80.) One verse sums up approximately 30 years of John's life; it was a time of preparation. There is a striking parallel which God seems to draw if we examine the lives of those who dramatically minister in a public way for God. Moses, Elijah, John, Jesus, Paul, all were removed, separated from society and its influences for a time. In that seclusion they heard God speak divine plans to their spirits. In their seclusion they could set their minds and souls on God in quiet contemplation.

John knew he was not the Christ, the Messiah, and gave testimony to that fact. *(Read John 1:15-28.)* John's ministry was to prepare the way for the Christ, to call the people to turn from sin and follow the Lord their God. He did a good job at this, and now John's time was coming to an end. *(Read John 1:29-34.)* John recognizes the one for whom he has been called to prepare the way. He encounters his Lord, his Messiah, the one he had proclaimed.

(Read John 3:22-30.) Here we hear John's final testimony before he is imprisoned. **Who is the bridegroom? Who is the friend of the bridegroom? Is the friend happy for the bridegroom?** John's disciples were envious of Jesus' success. They desired to see their master exalted, but in the kingdom of God there is no room for envy. God's people are called to work together rejoicing in the success each has as people turn to Jesus accepting salvation. John displays no envy or resentment.

His whole ministry was to prepare hearts to receive Jesus as Christ. His joy is full as he recognizes his Lord. Sent to bear witness to a greater one than himself, he faithfully discharges that compassion and gracefully steps aside so that Christ could have preeminence. And so begins the end of John's ministry.

John's message brought comfort to sinners as they received forgiveness in the waters of baptism but others were afflicted as they continued to live in their sin. John minced no words in dealing with the Pharisees, calling them a brood of vipers. There was no change in their hearts. Like Elijah and Elisha, John went up against the monarchy of his time, attacking Herod Antipas. The tetrarch of Galilee and Pera had sinned by marrying his niece, Herodias, who was already married to Herod's brother. Mosaic Law forbade this union. *(Read Leviticus 18:16.)* This couple found no joy in that voice crying in the wilderness. In fact, they desired to still his voice permanently and sought to do just that. *(Read Luke 3:19-20.)*

Once arrested, John's influence did not end. His disciples continued the work, and we see in Matthew 11:1-6 that the relationship between Jesus and John continues. *(Read.)* Languishing in prison for months, John seeks reassurance from Jesus. He questions if the work he has done and the work Christ is doing is producing results. He may have even hoped to urge Jesus to further action by his request. **Have you ever found yourself in need of this type of reassurance? What have been some of your thoughts and feelings? What does Jesus tell John's followers to do?** The healings of life-restoring miracles that they have seen and heard point to a God who fulfills his promises. This observable evidence adds proof to the predicted ministry of the Messiah as told in Isaiah. *(Read Isaiah 29:18-21, 35:5-6, 61:1.)*

Jesus' attention now turns to the crowd. *(Read Matthew 11:7-19.)* **What type of messenger did they seek? What type did they find?** John was unique. He was a prophet with a special role. A man of great character, his ministry was to announce what was at hand. John belonged to the old age covenant, preparatory to Christ. Yet just as the Jews of the

Old Testament rejected the covenant God made with them, so the Jews of the New Testament era would reject the covenant God was reaching out to establish with them through the blood of Jesus.

We see in Matthew 11:16-18 the reaction of the people to our two central characters. *(Read.)* John's message came as a funeral dirge to many ears, yet they did not want to dance to Jesus' tune either. The spiritually wise could see both ministries as valid and godly. Yet both were rejected. The King and herald would suffer violence at the hands of their own.

(Read Mark 6:14-29.) John is dead. The world had claimed the messenger. **Was John prepared for that final encounter with God?** We know from his words and ministry that he knew the God he served. **But did he become embittered over his circumstances? Was he frustrated with the people? Did he feel rejected by men and by God as he sat alone in jail? Did he feel abandoned, forgotten, spent? Have you ever found yourself in this situation? What were your feelings?**

John knew his mission was over. Messiah had come. John had been rejected. Jesus would be rejected. Hear the words of our Lord and take comfort as John must have in the promise of faithfulness to God. *(Read John 15:18-25.)*

John, the servant, knew the one who was greater, the master whose sandal he was not fit to untie. John knew the one who sent him and the one for whom he prepared the way. Those who lived in darkness chose to silence the voices of the two who spoke out against their sin. The miracles Jesus performed confirmed the fact that Messiah had arrived, the Day of Judgment had come, and so they stilled the voice of the one who called them to repent, John. And soon, they would silence the one who convicted them of their sin but offered new life, Jesus.

The world needs to hear again God's voice not to harden its hearts as the Israelites did. The world needs to hear again John's call to turn from its sin and embrace the Lamb of God, the only one who can take away sin. May our voices join and declare the glory of God to the world as we become God's voice and prepare for Christ's return.

Group Discussion Questions

Preparation of the Meal: God sends many messengers to speak to us throughout our lives.

What is the importance of baptism, Sunday school, confirmation, adult studies, worship, and so forth, in delivering that message?

Discuss how each may impact our faith formation.

Which one played an important part in your life?

Who delivered the message?

Share one person who impacted your faith journey and the way he or she did it.

Dish Up The Meal: A man stands on the corner with a placard, "Repent and Be Saved."

What would your reaction be to him?

Is it the message that upsets us or the messenger?

What is the importance of the way we deliver the Good News of salvation to others?

Have you ever been turned off by one of these messengers?

Have you ever been challenged to turn your life around and embrace faith in Christ? How did that happen?

Share the Meal: False prophets or true? Wacos or Billy Graham? People today are searching for the real meaning in life.

How do they get caught up in cults?

How can we discern false prophets from true ones?

John the Baptist spoke for God. Billy Graham is a recognized national leader today who we feel has credibility. Yet many so-called spiritual giants have tumbled in our time. What are the dangers in elevating people to pedestals?

Have you ever been let down by someone you thought was a spiritual giant?

How did you get over it?

What is the importance of prayer and Bible study in discerning who is speaking for God and who is leading one astray?

How might we help someone who seems to be headed onto the wrong path?

What kind of voices are our youth listening to today?

How might we help them to hear God's voice more clearly?

Beef Barley Soup Recipe

Cook one large soup bone with beef on in 2 quarts of water. Remove bone and shred meat. Add 1 cup chopped onion, 1 cup chopped celery, 1 cup diced carrots, 1 16-oz. can whole tomatoes, ⅔ cup barley, 1 teaspoon salt, ½ teaspoon paprika, ¼ teaspoon pepper, and chopped parsley. Bring to a boil, then lower heat. Cover and simmer 1 hour or until barley is tender. Add 1 envelope Lipton Soup mix with noodles. Cook 30 minutes longer.

*Soup recipe may be increased for a larger crowd. 1 cup chopped green pepper may be added also.

Jesus And Lamb Stew

Bible Study

Soups: Lentil, vegetable, chicken, potato, beef barley — foods we've enjoyed this Lent that have nourished the body. God's prepared: Jacob, Moses, Joshua, Elisha, John the Baptist — lives we've studied that have challenged the soul. In this Lenten Bread & Broth series, we have enjoyed the fellowship of sharing a meal and filling our minds with the study of God's Word.

Today we tasted lamb stew — a hearty soup filled with many nourishing items. Accompanying our meals have been breads. Bread is a staple in many diets, a food that nourishes and sustains us, a vital part of good nutrition.

We all enjoy a piece of fresh, homemade bread. A lot of preparation goes into making that delicious product. The smell and taste of freshly baked bread make our mouths water, so we make special efforts to prepare in order to partake of this delicious food.

Lent is a time of preparation. You have taken time to come together to study the Word, to prepare yourself. You will not be disappointed. God is pleased with your sacrifice. God has made a special sacrifice that we will examine in our concluding study: Jesus, the Bread of Life. Today we will look at how God prepared Jesus to be the body broken and the blood poured out as the sacrifice for our sins and prepared the world to receive this Lamb of God.

Even before the birth of God's Son, the prophet Isaiah foretold that birth and prepared the people. *(Read Isaiah 7:14,*

9:6-7.) **Who was this young woman who would bear this divinely conceived child?** *(Read Luke 1:26-38.)*

Last week we looked at John the Baptist's entrance into the world. God prepared the world for the messenger, the voice, the one who would prepare the way — the way for Jesus. Today we read of how God prepared Mary to receive Jesus. All of us are called to prepare our hearts and to give God consent to birth Jesus in our lives. **What was Mary's response? How might we prepare ourselves to allow God to birth Jesus in our lives?**

And so Jesus came into the world. *(Read Matthew 1:18-24.)* As with John, not much is known of Jesus' early life. As his ancestors were, Jesus was circumcised when he was a baby. *(Read Luke 2:21-23.)* **Why was circumcision important to the Jews?** Jesus was to live out his covenant relationship with God, preparing himself in all ways to be the true sacrificial lamb and the mediator of the new covenant. *(Read Hebrews 9:15.)* **Why was it necessary for God to make a new covenant with his people?** John came calling the people to remember that covenant and to turn from their sins. John had been prepared to deliver his message. Jesus was likewise prepared.

As with John, we also do not know much about the time Jesus went up with his family to the Temple as a lad until the beginning of his public ministry. *(Read Luke 2:41-51.)* **What type of preparation did Jesus' parents do for him? Why is it important to train up children in the ways of the Lord? What benefits does the body of Christ derive from such trained individuals?**

Jesus entered a time of earthly preparation — living out life in the routine of everyday living. Joseph was a carpenter, and Jesus probably spent lots of time observing him and learning the trade. But these years are unknown to us. We next see Jesus coming to John the Baptist for baptism. *(Read Mark 1:9-13.)* **Why was it important for Jesus to be baptized? Is it important for us today?** *(Read Matthew 28:19-20.)* **How is this commission fulfilled in the life of the church? What preparation is involved?**

Jesus has been circumcised and baptized. He has lived in the world and knows its struggles. He now enters his own spiritual struggle as the patriarchs before him did. Jesus is sent by the Spirit into the desert for a specific purpose. **What is that purpose?** *(Read Luke 4:1-13.)* **What were the temptations that came to Jesus?**

God allowed Jesus to be tempted in every way that all humankind is. He was tempted first to turn stone into bread: God calls his children not to be ruled by bribery. God takes care of his own. The God of the Old Testament is the same provider of today. *(Read Deuteronomy 9:2-10.)* God will give us our fill of bread if we walk in obedience to him. Jesus knew this. **How do we know this today? How can we experience God's providence and care?**

What was the second temptation, and what might we compare it with today? Obedience is key to a faithful walk with God. Jacob disobeyed and found himself living outside of the covenant relationship and away from the blessing of family. Moses disobeyed God by striking the rock and was not allowed to enter the Promised Land. The Israelites disobeyed God and wandered the wilderness for 40 years. Joshua and Elisha called the people to put away their foreign idols and worship and serve only God, but they continued to disobey and suffered the consequences. Jesus quotes Scripture to refute the devil's claim to authority. *(Read Deuteronomy 6:10-15.)* **How do we learn of God's ways? As informed believers, what is our responsibility?**

Satan failed to cause Jesus to depart from Scripture, so we find him in the last temptation seeking to tempt Christ by Scripture. **What is the final challenge Satan throws at our Lord?** *(Read Psalm 91:11.)* Compare this passage with Luke 4:10. Satan carefully omits the phrase "in all your ways." The Lord's way for Jesus was that of perfect dependence on God's perfect will. *(Read Hebrews 10:7, 9.)* **What was God's will for Christ?** *(Read Luke 4:14-19.)*

Jesus came to demonstrate God's love and grace. Having been prepared in the wilderness, Jesus began a public ministry like those before him by demonstrating the power of God. True light had broken into the darkness, but what was the result? *(Read John 1:9-13.)*

The world sought to snuff out that light. Jesus, like those prophets before him, met with opposition from the ruling authorities. They refused to believe that Jesus was the Son of God. Even the miracles that evidenced this were denied. *(Read John 9:24-34.)* When John was imprisoned, he sent his disciples to find out what fruit his ministry and Jesus' was accomplishing. Jesus' reply confirmed the fact that the kingdom had come: The eyes of the blind were being opened — not just the physically blind, but the spiritually blind. However, those so blinded did not want to see God in their midst. Guilt descended upon those who refused to see Jesus as the Messiah. *(Read John 9:35-41.)*

These Israelites were the descendants of Moses — those who had seen God in their midst and who had been fed in the wilderness. Yet they were the descendants also of those who had murmured against God and had tired of eating manna, God's heavenly bread. Now Israel was being offered bread again but was refusing to eat. *(Read John 6:30-36.)*

The Israelites perished in the desert because they had refused to trust and obey God. God's will for them was to take hold of his promises and enter into the Promised Land, but they continually murmured and refused to believe. **What is God's will for us, and how did Jesus plan to accomplish it?** *(Read John 6:38-42.)*

How is eternal life gained? Many try to gain eternal life through the law and good works, but eternal life is a gift from God — bought and paid for by the blood of Christ. God made a new covenant with Israel through that blood. God makes a covenant with us through our baptism into Christ's death and resurrection. As the Holy Spirit fell upon the prophets of old and equipped them for ministry and as the Holy Spirit fell upon Jesus empowering him to do the will of God, so we receive that same empowering. *(Read Hebrews 13:20-21.)*

66

Jesus stood before those he had come to die for and offered himself as the bread from heaven, but they continued to grumble. *(Read John 6:42-59.)* These passages sound cannibalistic to us. Indeed after the death of Christ, the Romans thought that the Christians actually were engaging in a type of flesh eating. They did not understand the concept of the body and blood. **How do we eat of Jesus today?**

The practice of Holy Communion began on the night of our Lord's preparation for death. In the breaking of bread and the sharing of the cup, Jesus instituted a means by which we could eat his flesh and drink his blood as a remembrance of that sacrifice he would be called to give. *(Read Luke 22:14-23.)* **What is the importance of the sacrament of Holy Communion?** Circumcision, baptism, communion are the external signs that we are living in a covenant relationship with God. The Israelites had broken their covenant with God through sin. It was necessary, therefore, that God made a new covenant with them through Jesus. This covenant was foretold by the prophet Jeremiah. *(Read Jeremiah 31:31-34.)* This new covenant is ours by faith. Israel was freed from the bondage of law by grace. We are freed by that same grace through Jesus, the Lamb of God. *(Read Galatians 3:23-29.)*

We find ourselves now having made a complete circle. God made a promise to Abraham to make him a mighty nation. We have journeyed in this Lenten study discovering how that promise has been received and how God's people have been prepared to claim it. God desires that no person will perish — that all will come to a saving knowledge of Jesus Christ. That takes time — times of preparation. God's Holy Spirit is at work in each of our hearts as baptized children of God. Jesus' work was accomplished on the Cross, but we serve and follow a living God. Jesus did not leave us to flounder around in this world trying to figure out what God desires. *(Read John 16:5-14.)*

What has God declared to you through this study? The Spirit of truth continues to speak to each of us preparing our hearts to receive Jesus. May our ears be continually open to

God's voice. May our eyes not be blinded by the world and its glory. May our minds be steeped in the Word so that we can rebuke the temptations that come our way with God's help. And may we daily walk in faithfulness, living out our covenant relationship with God through Christ Jesus our Lord. Amen.

Group Discussion Questions

Preparation of the Meal: "Come Away to a Quiet Place." That travel ad would catch our eyes for we are all people in need of a getaway.

What do you do to get away from the pressures and stresses in life?

Jesus was called to a getaway weekend. His wilderness experience was not such a great camping outing, however. Have you ever had a wilderness experience? Share.

How did that experience help you in life?

Dish Up the Meal: Temptations come in many forms. The serpent tempted Eve in the Garden, and she gave in. King Saul was tempted to offer sacrifice instead of waiting for the prophet Samuel to come, and gave in.

What is the consequence of giving in to temptation?

How did Jesus resist the temptation?

Have you ever been tempted?

How did you resist?

If you gave in, what might have helped you not to?

When we see a friend struggling with temptation, how might we help him or her to resist?

Share the Meal: Jesus resisted temptation, led a devout life, shared God's love, did miracles and helped many. Yet he was rejected.

How do you feel when you have done everything right and still get rejected?

What are some ways you have handled rejection?

What role does peer pressure have in your life?

When do you find yourself most vulnerable to temptation and rejection?

How do you handle it?

What is the importance of Jesus' example and the example of others in dealing with these issues? Share.

Lamb Stew Recipe

Cook 2 pounds cubed lamb shoulder until brown in ½ cup melted butter. Remove meat and brown 1 clove minced garlic and 2 chopped onions in remaining fat. Add 1 bay leaf, 3 tablespoons minced parsley, 2 teaspoons salt, ¼ teaspoon pepper and ½ cup tomato puree. Cook together for a few minutes. Place into deep kettle. Add 4 cups hot water and simmer covered for 1½-2 hours. Add 3 diced carrots, 1 diced small turnip, and 2 cups cubed potatoes and cook until vegetables are tender (about ½ hour).

*Recipe may be multiplied for use with larger groups.

Bread

Any homemade breads can be used with the meals including dinner rolls, onion bread, white bread, Italian bread, French bread, sourdough bread, hard rolls and so forth. Perhaps some members of the group have some specialty breads that they enjoy making or delicious bread recipes to share. Bakeries and specialty shops also carry wonderful breads that would complement the soups. The following are some tasty bread recipes which might be used with any of the Lenten meals.

Whole Wheat Bread

In a mixing bowl combine 2 cups whole wheat flour, ¼ cup sugar, 1 tablespoon salt and 2 packages active dry yeast. In saucepan heat until warm 2¼ cups milk and ¼ cup cooking oil. Remove liquid from heat and mix in 1 egg. Blend all into dry ingredients. Mix with beaters 30 seconds at low spead and 3 minutes at high speed. Mix in by hand 1 cup whole wheat flour and 3 to 4 cups white flour to form a soft dough. Knead 1 minute. Place in greased bowl and grease top of dough. Let rise until double (45 to 60 minutes). Punch down. Shape into 2 loaves and place in greased pans. Cover and let rise (30 to 45 minutes). Bake at 350° for 40 to 45 minutes. Loaf should sound hollow when tapped. Brush with melted margarine and remove from pans. Makes 2 loaves.

Round Graham Bread

Combine 1 cup warm water with yeast packet from a 13¾-oz. box of hot roll mix. Stir until yeast is dissolved.

Add ¼ cup melted butter or margarine, ½ teaspoon salt and 1 egg and stir until well blended. Add 1⅔ cups finely crushed graham cracker crumbs and flour mixture from hot roll mix; blend well. Cover and let rise in a warm place until double (about 1 hour). On a floured surface, knead dough until no longer sticky. Shape into a round loaf and place on a greased baking sheet. Combine 1 slightly beaten egg white and 1 tablespoon water; brush over bread. Sprinkle with 1 tablespoon of poppy seeds. Cover and let rise in a warm place until double (about 1 hour). Bake at 375° about 40 to 45 minutes. Makes 1 round loaf.

Pumpkin Bread

In large mixer bowl thoroughly combine 1½ cups all-purpose flour, 2 packages active dry yeast, ½ teaspoon ground ginger, ¼ teaspoon ground nutmeg, and ¼ teaspoon ground cloves. In saucepan heat ¾ cup milk, ¼ cup packed brown sugar, 2 tablespoons butter or margarine, and 1½ teaspoons salt just until warm, stirring constantly to melt butter. Add to dry mixture in mixer bowl; add ½ cup canned pumpkin. Beat at low speed with electric mixer for 30 seconds, scraping sides of bowl constantly. Beat 3 minutes at high speed. By hand, stir in ¾ cup raisins and 1¾ to 2 cups flour to make a moderately stiff dough. Knead on lightly floured surface until smooth and elastic (5 to 8 minutes). Shape into ball. Place in a greased bowl and turn once. Cover and let rise in warm place until double (about 1 hour). Punch down; cover and let rest 10 minutes. Shape into loaf; place in greased loaf pan. Cover and let rise until double (about 30 minutes). Bake at 375° for 35 to 40 minutes. Remove from pan; cool. Makes 1 loaf.

Pumpernickel Bread

Soften 3 packages active dry yeast in 1½ cups warm water. Combine 2¾ cups rye flour, 1 cup all-purpose flour, ½ cup dark molasses, 2 tablespoons shortening, 1 tablespoon cara-way seed, 1 tablespoon salt and softened yeast; beat well. Stir in 1½ to 1¾ cups all-purpose flour to make a stiff dough. Knead on lightly floured surface until smooth (8 to 10 minutes). Shape into ball. Place in greased bowl and turn once. Cover and let rise until double (about 1½ hours). Punch down and divide in half. Let rest 10 minutes. Shape into 2 balls. Place on greased baking sheet sprinkled with cornmeal. Cover and let rise until double (30 to 45 minutes). Bake at 375° until well browned, about 30 to 35 minutes. Remove from baking sheet; cool. Makes 2 loaves.

Herb Loaf

In large mixer bowl combine 1½ cups all-purpose flour, 1 package active dry yeast, 2 teaspoons dried celery flakes, 2 teaspoons dried parsley flakes, and ½ teaspoon dried, crushed thyme. In saucepan heat 1 cup milk, 2 tablespoons sugar, 2 tablespoons shortening, and 2 teaspoons onion salt just until warm, stirring constantly to melt shortening. Add liquid to dry mixture; then add 1 egg. Beat at low speed with electric mixer for 30 seconds, scraping bowl. Beat at high speed for 3 minutes. By hand, stir in 1½ to 2 cups all-purpose flour to make a moderately soft dough. Knead on lightly floured sur-face until smooth (5 to 8 minutes). Shape into ball. Place in greased bowl and turn once. Cover and let rise in warm place until double (about 1 hour). Punch down and let rest 10 minutes. Shape into a round loaf and place in a greased 9-inch pie plate. Cover and let rise until double (30 to 45 minutes). Bake at 375° for 30 to 35 minutes. Remove from pan and cool. Makes 1 loaf.

CPSIA information can be obtained
at www.ICGtesting.com
Printed in the USA
BVHW041916170222
629367BV00023B/537